super simple
seasHell Projects

FUN AND EASY CRAFTS INSPIRED BY NATURE

Kelly Doudna

Consulting Editor, Diane Craig, M.A./Reading Specialist

A Division of ABDO

ABDO
Publishing Company

visit us at www.abdopublishing.com

Published by ABDO Publishing Company, a division of ABDO, P.O. Box 398166, Minneapolis, Minnesota 55439.
Copyright © 2014 by Abdo Consulting Group, Inc. International copyrights reserved in all countries. No part of
this book may be reproduced in any form without written permission from the publisher. Super SandCastle™
is a trademark and logo of ABDO Publishing Company.

Printed in the United States of America, North Mankato, Minnesota
102013
012014

 PRINTED ON RECYCLED PAPER

Editor: Liz Salzmann
Content Developer: Nancy Tuminelly
Cover and Interior Design and Production: Kelly Doudna, Mighty Media, Inc.
Photo Credits: Kelly Doudna, Shutterstock

The following manufacturers/names appearing in this book are trademarks: 3M™, Americana® Multi-Purpose™,
Aleene's® Tacky Glue®, Crayola®, Clorox®, DAP®, Dawn®, Gold Medal®, Morton®, Reynolds®, Scotch®

Library of Congress Cataloging-in-Publication Data

Doudna, Kelly, 1963-
  Super simple seashell projects : fun and easy crafts inspired by nature / Kelly Doudna, consulting editor,
Diane Craig, M.A./reading specialist.
    pages cm. -- (Super simple nature crafts)
  Audience: Age 5-10.
  ISBN 978-1-62403-082-6
1. Shellcraft--Juvenile literature. 2. Nature craft--Juvenile literature. I. Title.
  TT862.D68 2014
  745.594--dc23
                        2013022904

Super SandCastle™ books are created by a team of professional educators, reading specialists, and
content developers around five essential components—phonemic awareness, phonics, vocabulary, text
comprehension, and fluency—to assist young readers as they develop reading skills and strategies and
increase their general knowledge. All books are written, reviewed, and leveled for guided reading, early
reading intervention, and Accelerated Reader® programs for use in shared, guided, and independent
reading and writing activities to support a balanced approach to literacy instruction.

to Adult Helpers

The craft projects in this series are fun and simple. There are just a few things to remember to keep kids safe. Some projects require the use of sharp or hot objects. Also, kids may be using messy materials such as glue or paint. Make sure they protect their clothes and work surfaces. Review the projects before starting, and be ready to assist when necessary.

Key Symbols

In this book, you will see some warning symbols. Here is what they mean.

 HOT!
You will be working with something hot. Get help!

 SHARP!
You will be working with a sharp object. Get help!

 ADULT HELP
Get help! You will need help from an adult.

contents

super seashells

We love the smell of the ocean. We love hearing the ocean in a seashell. Take a walk on the beach. Look for shells the waves left behind. Fill up your pail with the shells you find. Now it's time to get creative! Try the fun and simple projects in this book. Nature made the seashells. You can make the crafts!

about seashells

Humans and fish have skeletons inside their bodies. But many sea creatures wear their skeleton on the outside. We call this skeleton a shell.

The creature that lives in the shell is a **mollusk**. It needs the shell for protection. It makes the shell by using **minerals** it gets from seawater. The shell is left behind when the mollusk dies. This is what you find on the beach.

SEASHELLS IN THIS BOOK

These are some of the seashells we used for the projects in this book.

clam shell   clam shell   scallop shell   clam shell   coral

conch shell   cone shell   nutmeg shell   Babylon shell   cone shell   horn snail shell   cone shell

top shell   auger shell   olive shell   cowrie shell   nerite shell   moon snail shell   horn snail shell   brain coral   sand dollar

We used different sizes of seashells in this book.

TINY
less than
1 inch
(2.5 cm)

SMALL
about
1 inch
(2.5 cm)

MEDIUM
about 2 inches
(5 cm)

LARGE
3 inches (7.6 cm)
or larger

WHat you'll need

Here are many of the things you will need to do the projects in this book. You can find some of them around the house or outside. You can get others at a craft store or hardware store.

seashells

rubber gloves

small shovel

scissors

old toothbrush

small tin

beach picture

foam brush

ruler

stick

sandpaper

foil pie tin

parchment paper

pencil

paper clip

baking sheet

bleach

bucket

wooden stir stick

paper towels

dish soap

drill and ³⁄₃₂-inch
(8 mm) bit

white or nylon thread

raffia

small glass bottle

hot glue gun
and glue sticks

ribbon

sand

flat marbles

two-sided tape

shadow box frame

paper

empty soup can

acrylic paint

white air-drying clay

large bowl

plaster of paris

waterproof sealer

oven mitt

clay flower pots

gems

craft glue

all-purpose flour

salt

preparing seashells

Before you make the projects in this book, clean your seashells. Use one of the methods below. Then your shells will be ready to use.

Bleach Method

This is a popular way to clean shells. But bleach is a **dangerous** chemical. Have an adult help you with steps 1 through 4.

1 Have an adult mix equal amounts of bleach and water in a glass bowl.

2 Put on the rubber gloves. Gently put the shells in the bowl. Try not to splash the water and bleach.

3 Let the shells **soak** for a few hours. You will see flakes coming off the shells. Wait until all of the flakes have floated away.

4 Rinse the shells in clean water.

5 Use an old toothbrush to **scrub** away any dark flakes that are still on the shells. Rinse the shells again in clean water.

6 Lay the shells on paper towels. Let the shells dry.

WHAT YOU'LL NEED

rubber gloves
bleach
water
glass bowl
seashells
old toothbrush
paper towels
small shovel
ruler
dish soap

Burying Method

Ants and other **critters** will eat your shells clean!

1 Get **permission** to dig a hole somewhere in the yard. Make a hole about 18 inches (45.7 cm) deep.

2 Put the shells in the hole. Cover them with dirt.

3 Mark the spot. That way you can find it later.

4 Leave the shells in the dirt for a few weeks or even a couple of months. The longer you leave the shells buried, the cleaner they will be.

5 Dig up the shells.

6 Wash the shells in warm, soapy water. Let them dry.

Pro tip

Use empty egg cartons, paper plates, and zipper bags to sort your shells.

Pro tip

Some of the projects are messy. Protect your work surface with newspaper.

fun fact

The flaky coating on a shell is called the periostracum (per-ee-oh-stray-cuhm). *Periostracum* means "around the shell." It helps protect the shell. It is usually a lot darker than the shell.

Dangling Decorations

These delicate danglers will dress up any room.

WHAT YOU'LL NEED

baking sheet

paper

36 medium or small shells

1 large shell

drill and $3/32$-inch (8 mm) drill bit

ruler

white or nylon thread

scissors

12-inch (30.5 cm) stick

raffia

Before You Begin

1 Plan your shell strings. Lay them out on the baking sheet and paper. You'll need four strings with five shells for the mobile. You'll need four strings with four shells for the wall hanger.

2 Have an adult drill small holes in the large shell. Drill four holes around the edge of the shell. Drill two holes in the top of the shell ¼ inch (.6 cm) apart.

3 Look at the other shells you plan to use. See which ones you won't be able to tie a thread to. Have an adult drill a hole in each of these shells.

Mini Mobile

1 Cut five 24-inch (61 cm) pieces of thread.

2 Tie a small shell to one end of one piece of thread.

3 Tie another shell to the thread 3 inches (7.6 cm) from the first shell.

4 Add three more shells to the thread. Use five shells total. Space them all about 3 inches (7.6 cm) apart.

5 Follow steps 2 through 4 to make three more shell strings.

6 Tie one shell string through each of the four holes along edge of the large shell.

7 Tie the last piece of string through the two holes in the top of the large shell. Use it to hang your mobile.

Wall Hanger

1. Cut four 24-inch (61 cm) pieces of thread.

2. Tie a small shell to one end of one piece of thread.

3. Tie another shell to the thread 3 inches (7.6 cm) from the first shell.

4. Add two more shells to the thread. Use four shells total. Space them all about 3 inches (7.6 cm) apart.

5. Follow steps 2 through 4 to make three more shell strings.

6. Tie the shell strings to the stick. Space them evenly.

7. Cut a 16-inch (41 cm) piece of raffia. Tie one end to each end of the stick. Use it to hang your wall hanger.

small Bottle

This small bottle will make a big impression.

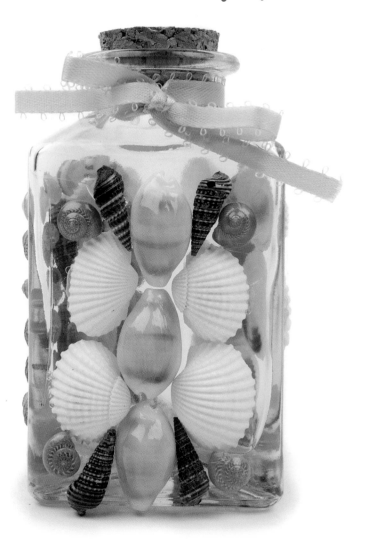

WHAT YOU'LL NEED

small glass bottle

tiny or small seashells

hot glue gun and glue sticks

ribbon

scissors

1 Lay the bottle on the work surface.

2 Put a dab of hot glue on the back of a seashell.

3 Stick the shell to the bottle.

4 Continue gluing on shells until the bottle is covered.

5 Tie a ribbon around the top of the bottle.

 Pro tip

If your bottle is round, Lay it on a towel to hold it in place. Then it won't roll while you are working on it.

BEACH SCENE

A tiny tin makes a delightful decoration.

1. Find a beach picture in a magazine. Set the tin upside down over the picture. Trace around the tin. Cut out the picture. It should fit in the bottom of the tin.

2. Tape the picture in the bottom of the tin.

3. Hot glue a paper clip to the top of the back of the tin.

4. Hold the tin at an angle. Pour some sand into the tin.

5. Put some shells and flat marbles on top of the sand.

6. Add a few dots of glue around the inside of the top of the tin. Close the tin. Slowly stand the tin up. Let glue dry.

fun tip

If you have been to the beach, use your own picture for a personal touch.

SHADOWBOX

Your shells will look fabulous in this fantastic frame.

WHAT YOU'LL NEED

shadow box frame at least 2 inches (5 cm) deep

medium, small, and tiny shells

paper

1. Lay the frame face down with the glass on the table. Remove the back of the frame.

2. Lay some **medium** shells in the frame.

3. Fill in the rest of the space with small and tiny shells.

4. Wad up some paper. Pack it in the frame behind the shells. This will keep them from moving around.

5. Replace the back of the frame.

6. Stand the frame up. Gently shake it to settle the shells.

7. If the shells move around too much, add more shells. Repeat steps 3 through 6.

 **Pro tip**

Gently lay the shells on the glass. Pick shells up to move them. This will help keep the glass from getting scratched.

pencil cup

A clay-covered can makes a colorful pencil cup.

WHAT YOU'LL NEED

shells

acrylic paint

foam brush

white air-drying clay

empty soup can, washed and dried

1 Paint some shells. Let the paint dry.

2 Prepare the clay according to the instructions on the package. Press the clay all around the can. Make a layer of clay ⅜ inch (1 cm) thick.

3 Press the painted shells into the soft clay. Let the clay harden completely.

 Pro tip
You may find it easier to roll out the clay before you press it to the can.

 Pro tip
Cracks may form as the clay hardens. Gently smooth them back together.

garden decoration

This pretty plaster pie will look great in the garden.

WHAT YOU'LL NEED

baking sheet

paper

pencil

seashells

other decorations, such as flat marbles

large bowl

plaster of paris

water

wooden stir stick

foil pie tin

sandpaper

waterproof sealer

foam brush

1. Trace around the pie tin on a piece of paper. Place the paper on a baking sheet. Arrange your shells on the circle. Add other decorations. Create a **design** you like.

2. Have an adult help mix the plaster of paris. Use 4 cups plaster of paris and 2 cups water. Stir with the wooden stir stick.

3. Pour plaster into the pie tin. Make it 1 inch (2.5 cm) deep.

4. Wait 4 or 5 minutes until the plaster is just starting to set.

5. Work fast to press the seashells and other decorations into the plaster.

6. Let the plaster harden according to the instructions on the package.

7. Pop the plaster out of the tin. Sand the edges if they are rough. Let the plaster finish hardening. Brush on a coat of sealer.

 **Pro tip**
The plaster will need two or three days to fully harden and dry.

23

flower pot

You'll be pleased to place your plants in these pots.

WHAT YOU'LL NEED

clay flower pots

hot glue gun and glue sticks

scallop shells

other shells (optional)

white acrylic paint (optional)

sponge (optional)

1 Hot glue a row of scallop shells around the top of the pot.

2 Hot glue another row of shells just below the first row. Fit the new shells between the shells in the row above.

3 Add more rows of shells until the pot is covered. Let the glue dry.

random and rugged variation

1 Hot glue larger shells onto the pot first. Arrange them in a **random design**.

2 Add smaller shells in the spaces between.

weathered look variation

1 Add a little water to white paint. Use a sponge to dab it around the pot. Let the paint dry.

2 Hot glue shells around the top of the pot.

SHALLOW DiSH

Show off your tiny treasures in a shallow shell dish.

WHAT YOU'LL NEED

acrylic paint

foam brush

4 tiny shells

large shell

hot glue gun and glue sticks

craft glue

small gems

1. Paint the outside of each tiny shell with one color. They will be the feet of the dish.

2. Paint the outside of the large shell a different color. Paint the inside white. The large shell will be the dish. Let the paint dry.

3. Arrange the four tiny shells in a square with the painted side up. Put a dab of hot glue on each one.

4. Set the large shell on top of the tiny shells. The white side should face up.

5. Put a thin line of craft glue around the rim of the large shell. Add small gems all the way around. Let the glue dry.

 **Pro tip**

If the paint is a light color, you might need to apply more than one coat.

PAPerWeigHt

Keep papers in place with this wonderful weight.

WHAT YOU'LL NEED

2 cups all-purpose flour

1 cup salt

½ cup sand

large bowl

1 cup water

tiny, small, and medium shells

baking sheet

parchment paper

oven mitts

Sand Dough

1 Put the flour, salt, and sand in the bowl.

2 Mix with your hands.

3 Add the water. Mix with your hands until the **dough** is smooth.

 **Pro tip**

Add a little more water if your dough is too dry.
Add a little more flour if your dough is too sticky.

Paperweight

1 Make a ball of sand **dough** about the size of a **tennis** ball.

2 Flatten the ball slightly with your hand.

3 Firmly press some shells into the dough.

4 Put parchment paper on the baking sheet. Set your paperweight on the baking sheet. Bake at 200 **degrees** for about 3 hours.

5 Carefully remove the baking sheet from the oven. Let the paperweight cool completely.

conclusion

Aren't seashells great? You have let the beauty of nature come through with these wonderful seashell crafts. If you had fun, don't stop here. How else can you use seashells?

And check out the other books in the Super Simple Nature Crafts series. You'll find projects that use ice, leaves, pinecones, pressed flowers, and twigs. The ideas are endless!

glossary

critter – any animal.

dangerous – able or likely to cause harm or injury.

degree – the unit used to measure temperature.

design – a decorative pattern or arrangement.

dough – a thick mixture of flour, water, and other ingredients used in baking or to make clay.

medium – not the largest or the smallest.

mineral – a natural element that plants, animals, and people need to be healthy.

mollusk – an animal with a soft body and a hard shell, such as a clam or a snail.

permission – when a person in charge says it's okay to do something.

random – without any order, purpose, or method.

scrub – to clean by rubbing hard.

soak – to remain covered in a liquid for a while.

tennis – a game played by two or four players who use rackets to hit a ball over a net.